THE BATSFORD COLOUR BOOK OF
Yorkshire

H. E. Whitaker

B. T. BATSFORD LTD
LONDON & SYDNEY

First published 1975

Text © H. E. Whitaker 1975

Filmset by Servis Filmsetting Ltd, Manchester
Printed and bound in Hong Kong
by Dai Nippon Printing Co, (Hong Kong) Ltd,
for the publishers B. T. Batsford Ltd, 4 Fitzhardinge Street, London W1H 0AH and
23 Cross Street, Brookvale, N.S.W. 2100, Australia

ISBN 0 7134 3012 5

Contents

Acknowledgments

The Publishers wish to thank the following for permission to re-produce the photographs in this book:

Peter Baker for page 41
J. Allan Cash for page 17
Arthur W. Dick for page 25
John Edenbrow for pages 51, 53
Noel Habgood for pages 21, 37, 49
A. F. Kersting for page 29
T. Parker for pages 45, 59
Picturepoint for page 19
Clifford Robinson for pages 39, 61, 63
Kenneth Scowen for pages 31, 43
Spectrum for pages 23, 27, 33, 35, 47, 55, 57

Introduction

The Yorkshireman still retains a clear concept of his county. Despite the new local administrative boundaries, for him Yorkshire stretches from the River Tees in the North to the Humber and Trent in the South, and from the sea in the East, to west of the Pennines.

The Vikings based their boundaries on easily recognisable geographical features, rivers, a watershed and so on; they divided Yorkshire into *thridings* – thirds – which in the process of time became known as Ridings. Hence it is still far easier to describe the country's scenery by reference to the old boundaries.

Yorkshire is a land rich in variety and diversity. It is certainly not the industrial wasteland so easily believed by those who have never visited it. Its boundary is over a thousand years old, give or take a few square miles donated by Henry VIII, and it has at its centre a capital city far older than London. It has mountain landscape reminiscent of the lower Alps, of the Israeli limestone hills, of the Cotswolds. It has a sea coast reminiscent of Dover and of Devon but with sandy beaches the equal of any in north-west Europe.

To what do we owe this great diversity?

First of all the enormous variety of the underlying rocks which influence its topography. From the oldest to the most recent, there are samples of almost every type and age of rock formation we find in Britain and most of north-west Europe.

In the far west of the region are the shales and sandstone remnants of ancient primeval landscapes formed before there was any life on the surface of the globe. Overlying these are the limestones and sandstones of the earliest carboniferous period which now form the spine of the Pennine upland regions, and in their time were the basis of the ancient tropical swamps which gave us our coal measures. The coal-bearing strata dips below the plain of York but before the plain is reached occurs a ridge of magnesium limestone rock which exists elsewhere, in Normandy – it is known as Caen stone, and from which was built York Minster and the Houses of Parliament.

The Pennines are highest on their western side. Those to the north and west comprised of limestone rock present a different landscape from those of the southern and eastern Pennines, whose less soluble grits and sandstone have a more rugged appearance. Thus we have the wildness of the moors round Haworth, millstone grit moors, compared with the sweeping, though no less rugged, uplands of the Craven Pennines and the Dales at the head of Wensleydale and Swaledale, which in turn rise to those strange peaks Pen-y-gent, Ingleborough, Whernside and Mickle Fell.

The eastward-flowing Pennine streams were captured in comparatively recent times by the River Ouse. Thus the rivers Swale, Ure, Nidd, Wharfe, Aire, Calder and Don, flow together into the massive estuary of the Humber. The Tees only escaped such a fate by the intervention of mankind. More curious still is the River Derwent which rises five miles from the sea coast, then turns round and flows westwards through the Vale of Pickering, cuts its own gorge between the Howardian Hills and the chalk escarpment of the Wolds, and finally joins the River Ouse near where Selby now stands. Again, this is a trick of the Ice Age which cut off the Derwent from its natural outfall the sea, causing it to form a great lake which eventually overflowed into the Vale of York, and drained away to leave the wide, flat-floored plain of the Vale of Pickering which now separates the gently eastward-flowing slopes of the North Yorkshire Moors from the high north-facing escarpment of the Yorkshire Wolds. The Wolds themselves in turn descend gently from the escarpment to the Vale of Holderness.

Other glacial lakes formed in the central plain of York behind a mass of detritus stretching from the Wolds across the middle belt of Yorkshire to the Pennine foothills. It was this great moraine which provided the first great east-west route across the county, which together with the City of York which now stands upon it, shaped the county's genesis.

To the diversity of landscape must be added the diversity of human colonisation and development.

Today we find traces of Neolithic man on the hilltops and lake dwelling man in the former swamps. Near Flamborough are traces of Neolithic workshops from which flint implements were traded throughout the rest of the country. Ancient man fortified this headland with a steep ditch and earthworks now misleadingly known as Danes Dyke, but which were certainly in existence many thousands of years before the Danes appeared.

There are other traces of early man on the tops of the Pennines and indeed we find roads there which were in existence a thousand years before the Romans arrived. They are presently preserved as green tracks beloved of moorland hikers. The Phoenicians used them. They were well known to the Brigantes and the Parisi, this latter a tribe of pre-Roman settlers from the area where Paris now stands.

The Romans first gained a foothold in the north of England through a northern beauty, Queen Cartimandua of the Brigantes, who preferred an alliance with the Mediterranean intruders to one with her estranged husband. She sealed her bargain by delivering the defeated and refugee Caractacus to the Romans. In turn the Romans fortified the region, subdued the Brigantes, and established their settlements at Malton *(Derventium)*, from which the east coast was defended from marauding north-west Europeans; and York itself *(Eboracum)*, from which with its fortress of 6,000 troops the whole of the northern defence system was controlled.

Despite the importance of Roman occupation (no less than three Roman Emperors – Hadrian, Severus, and the most important of all, Constantine, visited York) all traces of those early occupations have succumbed to the weight of succeeding invasions. Even the place names are of later date. While London derives its name from the Romans, York is derived from Jorvik, the name of a Danish invader.

The Romans absorbed the ancient warlike Brigantes, so that when the Romans left, the residents, softened by years of good living, fell easy prey to the Angles and Saxon marauders, who in turn first colonised and then established their own civilisation.

The Saxons in their turn either defeated and repelled or absorbed the Pictish and Scottish invaders and established a Celtic Christian England. They defeated Penda of Wales and thoroughly established the basis of the religious communities of the north. They accepted Roman Catholicism at the great Synod of Whitby in the seventh century, but were later overcome by the Viking invaders – largely Danish – who eventually established a kingdom in England based in York.

The Anglo-Saxons re-established communities in the old Roman settlements, and their chief contribution to Yorkshire's landscape is in the multiplicity of religious centres they created. Most Yorkshire village churches can claim some connection with Saxon times. Their greatest monuments were the Abbey of St Hilda at Whitby, now standing stark above the moors, the colours of the sea forming patterns of ancient stained glass in its empty windows, and Ripon Cathedral.

A church dating from Saxon times on the site of the Roman barracks in York lies under the foundations of the present Minster. But the most intriguing Saxon remain is the tiny cell under Ripon Cathedral which was where St Wilfred established a ministry.

The Viking contribution is to be found in the patterns of many of our modern settlements, for example in the lay-out of the present walls of the city of York; in street names which are more often called 'gates' in older Yorkshire towns and villages after the Scandinavian *gatte* or *gatten*; and in dialect and local speech. The dialect of Flamborough is so closely akin to Danish that even today Danes and local Flamborians can understand each other, using respectively dialect and language.

Vikings also introduced a duality within the region which still persists. Whereas the Danes invaded the Yorkshire coast and spread inland, the Norwegians invaded the west coast and penetrated the Pennines. The Vikings were not above internecine squabbles. They fought each other in the central plain of York, after which the Pennines became totally inhabited by Norwegians and the great Danish Kingdom was established from the City of York.

This division is reflected in the pattern of settlement in the upland hills. So many of the ancient upland farms follow the style of Norwegian farmsteads. The practice of building barns in the fields, which adds such a distinctive feature to the landscape, is similar to present-day Norwegian practice. But there the similarity ends, for whereas the Norwegians build of wood the Yorkshire upland farms are of stone.

Even the older fishing boats, known as Cobles, and the style in which they are painted are direct descendants of the Viking long ships, though adapted for the hard task of beaching on a rough Yorkshire coast.

The great eras of the Saxons and Vikings may be said to have ended in Yorkshire. For it was in 1066 that Harold, last of the Saxon kings met Hardrada, king of Norway, at Stamford Bridge, seven miles from York and defeated him, slaughtering the Viking forces.

But William did not find the north too easy to conquer and it was not until 20 years later that William finally subdued these vigorous, robust northern people when he laid waste the north. Villages and towns were put to the sack. Men, women and children were slaughtered. For 200 years the country was impoverished. Yet during this period a start was made on the last of the great Minsters which now stands at York. Towns and villages struggled back to life. But a division had been created between the north and south of England which in many respects has lasted.

The north of England remained a battleground between English and Scottish troops until the end of the Tudor period. It is little wonder, then, that we find so many fortresses within the county. These range from the walled city of York fortified by William, and in which one of his earliest castles, Clifford's Tower still stands, to the castles of Wressle, Pontefract, Skipton, Middleham, beloved of Richard III, Castle Bolton, Richmond – of which it was said it was so strong it was never attacked, Malton – of which nothing remains, Helmsley, Pickering, Scarborough and the walled cities of Beverley and Hull.

Sheep-rearing over the Wolds, Moors and Pennines was suited to a depopulated countryside. When the Cistercian monastic order was established at Rievaulx and Fountains, sheep-rearing and wool trading fell into the hands of the church. Thus in the Vale of York, the North Yorkshire Moors and the foothills of the Pennines, we find the often beautiful remains of the old monastic churches. Two we have mentioned, but to those must be added Kirkstall, Jervaulx, Byland, Whitby itself, Kirkham, Roche and the still existing parish church which is half of the former Abbey at Bridlington. We are fortunate indeed that the Minsters of York and Beverley, the Abbey of Selby and the Cathedral of Ripon, still remain, and indeed that York Minster contains such a rich store of medieval glass despite the marauding commissions of Henry VIII and the stern Puritan destroyers of the Cromwell period.

But it is only in the old East Riding that we find the beautiful wool churches so reminiscent of those in East Anglia, the Cotswolds and southern England.

Hedon, to the east of Hull, and one of the oldest boroughs in England, has a church called the King of Holderness. Patrington a few miles away, has a fourteenth-century church whose delicacy of design and construction, and particularly its spires, gives it the title Queen of Holderness.

By the time of William a change had come over the landscape in Yorkshire. In the early days before the Romans, ancient routes had followed the hilltops above the swamps and impenetrable forests of the lowlands. Hence, before the Romans and again during the Anglo-Saxon and Viking periods, major routes in Yorkshire had tended to cross from east to west along the crest of the Wolds, and the great central moraine dividing the Vale of York, to the Pennines, and down to the west coast. Alternatively, they lead south to the Peak District and across to Wales, or down the great jurassic ridges towards the south-west, and the ultimate capital of England at Winchester. The Romans established their north-south routes for a short period. The Normans settled the capital of England on London, and routes radiated from it.

From this time, parts of Yorkshire became cut off from the beaten track. Thus the Pennine valleys, the North Yorkshire Moors and the Wolds themselves, tended to turn their backs on the Great North Road.

The important towns and settlements were located in the Vale of York. Other medieval settlements tended to draw in upon themselves and become remote. The sense of remoteness is still with us, and is reflected in intense parochial feelings in Yorkshire which help to give the Yorkshireman his independence.

But still the old divisions remain. To the old east-west division between the ancient Norwegians and Danes was now added the north-south division between Norman, Franco-England, and the border country that lay between the Humber and the Forth, fought over, and fortified; of great ecclesiastical wealth but poor in village life – an area of great landed estates, and hence a haven for the great medieval and Tudor families of the Court when the King's favours were removed.

The two Royal houses of York and Lancaster which fought the wars of the Roses, really represented a division between north and south. Yet in Yorkshire the Lancastrian House was represented by the great families of the plains and the east, and the Yorkist Houses by the families of the Pennines. Warwick the Kingmaker 'ruled' from his castle at Middleham. Richard III spent much time in Yorkshire at Pontefract, Middleham and York. But Harry Hotspur landed at Ravenspur on the Yorkshire coast.

Again, when England broke into the tumult of the Parliamentary wars of Charles I, it was the West Riding that provided General Fairfax and supported the Parliamentarian cause, while the East Riding and the Plain of York – particularly York itself – followed the King.

It is not surprising therefore that the great houses of Yorkshire tend to be either medieval and Tudor fortified houses, or the gracious mansions of the post-Cromwellian period. The latter are to be found in the eastern side and the Plain of York. This is not to say that there are many fine old stone houses built in the Dales and millstone grit moors of the old West Riding. But they are generally simpler, robust structures. Vanbrugh, by contrast, was chosen to design the magnificent palace of Castle Howard.

Yorkshire's landscape and beauty depend much on the pattern of human development, responsive to economic influences, and so are a product of history. The inter-action of this pattern of settlement on the landscape itself has produced the unique features, the diversity and the unity, which makes up the rural scene to a far greater degree than in those parts of Britain which have received the full impact of modern economic development, unrelated either to social or economic history.

Yorkshire's castles are exactly where you would expect to find them; each guarding a natural route or a river valley. Swaledale breaks into the Plain of Yorkshire through a narrow gorge which is crowned by Richmond Castle. Castle Bolton and Middleham are twin guardians of the broader Wensleydale, where dale meets the plains. The River Nidd squeezes itself into a narrow chasm on top of which we find Knaresborough Castle. Wressle Castle stands guard beside the Humber, Helmsley protects the narrow gap between the Hambledon and Howardian Hills, and which links the Vale of Pickering to the Vale of York.

The great ecclesiastical houses are generally hidden in the valleys.

Even the cities of West and South Yorkshire have grown out of early settlements in exactly the right positions, Leeds at a natural bridge point of the River Aire, Bradford at a route centre where the wool could be brought from the moors for trade with the early clothiers.

But it is in rural life that we see this essential harmony between Nature and Man. In the limestone Dales and northern Pennines, the stone walls are indicative of landholdings rather than animal enclosures. Indeed, the sheep roam free above walls on the moorland tops. To this is added the curious feature of the field barns, reminiscent of Norwegian agricultural practice, but making a major contribution to the scene.

Village populations are counted in scores and hundreds, and these tiny settlements cling to the bottom of the valleys, the houses huddled together for protection from the weather.

The landscape has contributed, too, to the pattern of human settlement for in the southern Pennines where the valleys are narrow and steep-sided, cut into the millstone grit, the villages form long ribbons on the sparse flat land along the valley bottoms or cling precariously to the hillsides.

Stone walls occur again, but here they are very different from those to be found in the Dales area. In the true millstone grit country we find large regular solid blocks, whereas the limestone tends to be less regular, scored with different patterns of the wall-builders art. Further south in the Pennines are finer sandstones, and walls, houses and buildings show the characteristic shallowness of the stone courses. Here too, among the older buildings, stone roofs of the easily split sandstone are common.

Along the ridges of creamier coloured limestone the villages are brighter, until, coming to the Wolds themselves, where chalk is often used, the whitest of limestones contrasts with the red pantiled roofs.

Throughout the Vales of York, Pickering and Holderness, brick is a predominant building material. However, the native brick of Yorkshire is burnt a darker colour than is found elsewhere, so that the city of York's streets and Georgian houses show a more autumnal tint than one would normally expect from brick buildings. Again, the colours fluctuate according to the clays and marls from which the brick was made.

The key to Yorkshire lies in the city of York itself. From whichever direction one approaches it, the roads are built on the tops of the old morainic materials and yield panoramic views. But the horizons of Yorkshire are always bounded by hills. As one drives north into the county, to the west lie the rising foothills of the Pennines. But on a clear day, the sharp edge of the Wolds appears like a faint blue line in the distance, a backdrop to the towers of York Minster.

York should be a pedestrian city. The walls, in which all the original bars still exist in beautiful preservation, enclose an area about one-third the size of Hyde Park. It is by no means a museum piece. Within the walls are examples of every kind of townscape from ancient to modern times, happily jostling together; medieval, Tudor, Georgian, Victorian, alongside Elizabethan and Stuart, and here and there even a modern housing estate. But everywhere one catches glimpses of the Minster; glance upwards from the modern array of a boutique established in a Victorian shop and there is seen a pinnacle, a tower, a gleaming reminder of the city's history. A few steps away from the modern Marks & Spencer's is The Shambles, the ancient street of the butchers, where the overhanging upper storeys almost preclude all light and air, but offer shelter to the housewife. Whip-ma-Whop-ma Gate is probably the shortest street in Britain, hardly longer than its name.

13

But I suggest you strike out from York, still following the ancient morainic route which leads eastwards to that ever beckoning blue line of hills, the Yorkshire Wolds. As you climb the escarpment, look back over the plain towards the cities and towns of Yorkshire – York, Selby, Pontefract, Leeds.

If you look forward you see an entirely different country, where the roads stretch in long, straight lines with wide grass verges; where each small hill is crowned with an artificial-looking coppice. The hedgerows are disappearing fast, falling to the mechanised agricultural methods of modern day. But before they do, we should remember that this countryside owes all to the agricultural reformers of the eighteenth century who laid their own pattern on a wilderness.

Not far from the top of the escarpment, midway between Garrowby Hill and Driffield, a delicate spire poking through the trees announces the presence of Sledmere, home of the Sykes family, eighteenth-century leaders in agricultural reform who decided that when their lands were enclosed they would leave common land alongside the roads, thus giving us today's wide grass verges. They enclosed their fields with thick hedges, planted the coppices on the hilltops and shelter belts of trees around every farm on their estate.

It is recorded that the average temperature of the region was raised by some 2° simply by these methods. Arable farming, barley, oats, sugar beet and turnips certainly became possible after their reforms and herds of pedigree sheep replaced their almost wild predecessors.

Or choose again the road to the east, but this time follow the edge of the escarpment, along the Hull Road, through Pocklington and Market Weighton where the road again climbs slowly over that escarpment, where settlements and houses fall away until, from the ridge, one catches yet another of Yorkshire's glorious views. This time in the distance we see an edifice which seems to aspire to the glories of York Minster. Here, the country gives a hint of the heathlands around Newmarket, and with good reason, for centred on the racecourse at Beverley are several training stables. Around Beverley too we find another historical remnant in the great open common lands surrounding the town. Today, they are green and well-wooded parkland, perpetually preserved for the enjoyment of the inhabitants. Harrogate shows a similar feature, the famous Strays which surround and hem in the little grey town on the western side of Yorkshire.

Outside the city walls, along a road appropriately named North Bar Without, we find again the Regency and Georgian mansions set back from the road and secluded among the trees, so reminiscent of York. North Bar is the only remaining city gate and inside it the street opens out into a wide market square, with a canopied market cross. It is a reminder of the many market towns built in this fashion throughout Yorkshire. The market places vary from an extra wide village street as at Yarm, Guisborough, Pocklington and Market Weighton, to the totally enclosed square as in Beverley, Thirsk, Richmond and so on. They all remind us that the great agricultural activity in Yorkshire has always been animal husbandry and these open spaces held the pens for sheep fairs, cattle markets and horse fairs – some remnants of which still remain.

Beyond Beverley the name of Kingston-Upon-Hull is a reminder that the port owes its genesis to the great ransom, largely paid in wool, for Richard the Lionheart when he was imprisoned in Sicily. The contribution levied upon the Yorkshire monasteries and landowners was shipped from the wharves alongside the river Hull where it meets the Humber, and from then on, Hull became an export centre for the early medieval wool trade. Like Beverley, this was a walled and fortified city, one of the few in the eastern side of Yorkshire which closed its gates to King Charles I. The moats were chosen as a line for many of the docks.

At the mouth of the river the land which has swept on downwards from the Wolds until it lies only a few feet above sea level, finally, reluctantly gives way to the sea in a long, thin, curving strip of shingle beach at the end of which stands Spurn Lighthouse.

Spurn is an end for Yorkshire, but also a beginning. Where does Yorkshire begin or end? Perhaps in the heart of a Yorkshireman for whom his county is more like a country in its variety, contrast and harmony.

YORK: THE CITY WALLS

The walls are medieval but stand on mounds raised by Normans, Vikings and Saxons of earlier times. The original Roman city walls are located on the east bank of the river and remnants may be seen close to York Minster itself.

The townscape is preserved because it fulfils a useful function in modern life. No buildings may be constructed higher than the average existing roof levels so that the relationship between Minster, walls and city is preserved. Banquets still take place in the Merchant Adventurers' Hall.

The Minster broods over the city. It overwhelms the tiny streets. It is a focus of attention. It presents a panorama of light and colour and fragile stonework, and it contains monuments to innumerable citizens of the 250 years in which it was built. Its presence is felt in every nook and cranny of the city and it imposes its welcome presence wherever one might be, continuing to fulfil its original spiritual purpose.

The view from the city walls is by no means that of a museum town. It is a living townscape taking its rightful place in the twentieth century.

YORK: THE GUILDHALL

York too was a major wool-exporting city of the medieval period, and its river was lined with wharves and quays. The wharves are still there, the barges still transport agricultural produce and bulky cargoes to this day. But fishermen line its banks, and river trips start from the little staithes alongside Lendal Bridge close to the Guildhall.

The Guildhall itself, rebuilt after wartime bomb damage, is surrounded by original and older buildings. Behind the four windows of the single-storied section in this photograph, King Charles I was sold by the Scots to the Parliamentarian Forces, the City Fathers acting as honest brokers and taking their percentage. Nowadays in the same room the descendant City Fathers fix the rate, no doubt wishing that the event could be repeated to provide them with some relief.

The larger windows on the left indicate the York City Council chambers. Behind this group of buildings is a perfect Georgian Mansion House, official home of the Lord Mayor of York, who is required to live in it during his year of office.

BISHOP BURTON

The rural characteristics of the Yorkshire Wolds are epitomised in villages such as Bishop Burton. The decline in rural population during the second half of the twentieth century has relieved these communities of major pressures for extra housing. Hence their character has fortuitously been preserved.

When the mid-eighteenth century agricultural reforms took place in the Wolds it became a more common practice than is generally the case in rural Yorkshire, for farms to be built in the villages, so that today we often see a curious mixture of Georgian rural architecture and farm buildings grouped usually around the village pond, but often incorporating an ancient chestnut, elm or oak tree.

Thus, there are typically Georgian houses with portico doors, small paned windows and very often a dairy or even a stable forming an addendum to the frontage, and in a by-road off the main village square, the farm workers' cottages. This picture of an integrated working landscape is similar in origin to that of York's working townscape, where a handsome town house is often surrounded by workshops or warehouses. Its houses are meticulously painted and preserved, reflecting their owners' pride in their dwelling as a working home.

If there is an emphasis on the village pond it is because the chalk of the Wolds was so porous that water supplies had to be husbanded. One may still see Dew Ponds created in the fields where the farmer has dug out a shallow depression, lined it with puddled clay and left it to accumulate water from rainfall and heavy dews.

BEVERLEY MINSTER

If York Minster's low bulk broods over the city, Beverley's fifteenth-century spires climb to the heavens.

There is no clear definition of 'a minster'. However, there *are* many characteristics which have come to be associated with them. They were certainly centres of learning. The international fame of Bishop Alcuin of York was, for example, so great that he was invited to the Court of Charlemagne to found the Emperor's system of ecclesiastical teaching at Aachen in Germany. St John of Beverley was another medieval cleric of wide educational influence.

These major churches never had a monastery and one often finds an Abbey close by whose priests served the requirements of the major church. Hence, close to the west end of York Minster lies the ruins of St Mary's Abbey. Close to Beverley lies another St Mary's still in use, that is like a cathedral in its proportions.

Size was not the criterion, however, for in Yorkshire two at least of the smallest parish churches are designated Minsters.

For many, the proportions and delicacy of architectural detail of Beverley Minster are more attractive than York itself.

BRIDLINGTON

Bridlington, encircled by the Wolds and white chalk cliffs, is framed in a sheltered bay. On-shore summer breezes can raise a rough sea, but even though west and northerly winds may reach gale strength, the waters are usually smooth.

It is a town composed of three ancient settlements whose history long precedes the days of the holidaymaker. One village owed its existence to the ancient priory, of which roughly no more than half still stands, together with its bayle gate. An ancient street of Georgian and Victorian house and shop frontages is in character with the towns and villages of the Wolds. Its position over a mile from the coast allowed an early warning system against Viking and Saxon marauders.

On the coast, however, where a 'misfit' stream drains the Great Wold Valley and forms the tiny estuary to the sea there grew up two other villages: Hilderthorpe, a fishing village and later shipbuilding and merchanting town, which merged very swiftly with the other settlement of Bridlington Quay.

FLAMBOROUGH: THE NORTH LANDING

You can find red chalk in Yorkshire which is a reminder that England's white chalk cliffs were formed in placid seas bordered by red desert sands from which the winds blew a stream of deposits. Hence, close to Flamborough the chalk is coloured red from the remains of the sand.

Yorkshire's chalk is from the base of the chalk formations. Much later, the glaciers deposited masses of clay over the old cliffs. One further feature of Yorkshire's white cliffs is the way in which the end grain of the rock is presented to the sea, so that the sea's constant fretting at the base of the cliff results in an outline which resembles a herd of white elephant bull heads.

Coves and inlets have been explored by the ever-encroaching fingers of the sea, which has widened the natural fissures into caves rivalling in size the interiors of some of Yorkshire's ancient churches. Similarly, the fissures at Bempton provide the ledges on which a myriad of protected seabirds make their nesting place.

Flamborough, or Flayneburg to use its early medieval name, has always been a navigator's beacon. It was here that John Paul Jones, a renegate Scot, the first Admiral of the American Navy, met an English squadron and defeated it. He was after the rich haul of merchant shipping which made its call at Flamborough on its way down the eastern coast of England.

CASTLE HOWARD

'Nobody had informed me that at one view I should see a palace, a town, a fortified city, temples on high places, woods worthy of being each a metropolis of the Druids, the noblest lawn in the world fenced by half the horizon, and a mausoleum that would tempt one to be buried alive; in short, I have seen gigantic palaces before, but never a sublimer one.'

So wrote Horace Walpole of Castle Howard. Yorkshire has long been the home for many of England's greatest families – the Percys, the Earls of Carlisle, the Howard family, closely related to the Norfolk family, of which one famous member was Catherine Howard, fifth ill-fated wife of Henry VIII; the Cliffords, Halifax, Harewoods, Devonshire – even Warwick the Kingmaker, *éminence grise* of the Wars of the Roses, had estates and a castle at Middleham.

Castle Howard was started by the 3rd Earl of Carlisle on the site of an older castle, in 1699. It was the first great building (1699–1726) by Sir John Vanbrugh (though much, including the famous mausoleum, is by Nicholas Hawksmoor). Walpole has said all about Castle Howard but only hints how, under Vanbrugh's courageous interpretation, this whole project utilises the surrounding countryside in the majesty of its conception.

SCARBOROUGH

Scarborough, standing between an escarpment and the sea, presents panoramas of itself, of the moors, and of the coast. One of the vantage points is the ancient harbour walls, from which the town is seen to be framed by hills which overspill their trees and pastures into the town itself.

Dividing the town is another escarpment crowned by the remains of fortifications which have variously existed since Roman times. From here the coast as far as Boulby Ness can be seen to the north and as far as Flamborough Head to the south.

The early fortifications were sacked and burned by the Vikings. The medieval structure became the home of Piers Gaveston, unfortunate friend of Edward II. Its owners took sides in the Wars of the Roses, and was bombarded during the Parliamentary wars by Cromwell from a hill across the bay which now bears his name – Oliver's Mount.

On the opposite side of the South Bay the discovery of a mineral spring in 1680 founded Britain's earliest medicinal resort and Scarborough's future holiday importance. The Spa, an architecturally unimpressive building, stands at the foot of well-wooded cliffs on top of which are the more graceful crescents and terraces of magnificent Georgian and early Victorian hotels.

ROBIN HOOD'S BAY

North from Scarborough successive escarpments of the North York Moors end in a series of headlands between which the sea has eroded much larger bays than are to be found further south at Flamborough. Beneath the sea's surface long spurs of rock run out into the bays. Usually at some vantage point, a river bed or a break in the cliffs, occurs a village such as Robin Hood's Bay close to Whitby.

The village clings precariously to a cliff face and has had to be supported by massive sea protection structures in recent years. Its 'streets' are no wider than is required by one fisherman to carry a basket of fish on his back. A road meanders down from the moors, twisting its way amongst the houses, and loses itself on a slipway to the beach.

Like so many of the bays and inlets along this coast, it formed a trap for sailing ships when the wind switched round to the south or east. It is said that one of these vessels, in its last extremity, tossed its bowsprit into the window of an inn facing the sea, thus allowing its crew to escape into the comfort of the bar!

There are numerous legends surrounding the name of the village, but whatever Robin Hood is supposed to have done, it is clear that he used this area as a refuge when the pace became too hot for him.

WHITBY

Standing on the high ground between Robin Hood's Bay and the Valley of the River Esk, are the remains of yet another monastic centre, St Hilda's Abbey of Whitby. It was a site that once again might not have satisfied modern planners, but its 'intrusion' onto the moor focuses attention, and contributes to the visual impact of an otherwise unrelieved landscape.

The Abbey was the scene of a great Synod in the 7th century when the Celtic and Catholic faiths in England were reconciled. Here too, in the stables, some of the first literary works in the English language were written by Caedmon.

Shipbuilding and whaling were once followed at Whitby, but they have now all but disappeared. A small shipyard remains in the upper harbour, and fishermen still use the port, but now they seek the rich harvest of the inshore fishing grounds.

The holiday industry developed after the difficulties of building rail connections to Whitby had been overcome. Its contribution of the Victorian hotels is found on the west side of the town, since it must be remembered that the River Esk flows north into the sea.

It would be unusual if a town with these traditions had not made its mark in our times, and indeed, through the navigational skills required of the whaling fraternity and early shipping interests, the region produced no less than three important navigators, of whom Captain Cook, born at Marton in Cleveland, and apprenticed first in Staithes and then in Whitby, is the greatest.

STAITHES

Still moving northwards, not far from the highest cliffs in England at Boulby Ness, Staithes is yet another characteristic coastal community, totally enclosed within the narrow confines of a river valley, looking to the sea for its income, turning its back sharply on the land. Notice that where the building space is restricted the houses often mount to three full storeys and pay little attention to street plans. With inadequate space they form a jumble and streets turn into alleyways.

These communities depended totally on fishing for their economy until very recent times. The industry's pattern varied with the season – line fishing in winter, crab and lobster in the spring, herring in late summer and early autumn. Fish for sale outside their community had to be carried long distances on animal packs to the inland market towns, or exported to Europe; it was therefore salted or smoked (Whitby kippers are still famous).

The only other industry of significance owing everything to the remoteness of the villages, was illicit – smuggling!

The long protruding reefs which were death traps for unsuspecting sailing ships offer harbour-like protection for those who know how to use them and are often laid bare at low tide. At Staithes the typical fishing vessel departs from the coble design. They are largely inshore boats and have an eye on the rich salmon harvest of autumn.

STOKESLEY

Turning away from the enclosed communities of the coast, the roads are devoid of settled communities until one crosses the Cleveland Hills and comes down into the great plain of the River Tees.

Nestling close under the hills we find a succession of country towns, Marton, Great Ayton, Eston and Stokesley, often sited on a river bank which in turn has broken a way through the hills from whence comes the farming community to market its animals.

Stokesley is such a town. It now begins to suffer – or enjoy – the invasion of businessmen with rural ambitions, from the great industrial areas around Teesside. It is their arrival which explains the somewhat awkward-looking single-storey garages constructed between houses in a village street, in spaces from which a cottage has vanished.

Such intrusion may be deplored, but it does underline the fact that the rural communities have declined in population and economic value in recent years. The advent of a fresh purpose could do much to preserve the character of these towns – and many of them have features certainly well worth preserving.

RIPON CATHEDRAL: THE WEST FRONT

Due west from York a road leads to Ripon, gateway to Nidderdale, which in turn is gateway to the Yorkshire Dales. Here is another of Yorkshire's great ecclesiastical houses, only the fifth building in stone to be built in the Saxon world. At the time of St Wilfred its founder it was said to be the most important stone building in Europe.

It presents a curiously stunted appearance from the outside, but its interior is one of the tallest in England, the nave being over 90 feet in height. Its somewhat squat appearance is partially due to the fact that the towers have lost their spires.

Stylistically it forms a text book of early architecture in stone, having contributions from the Saxon, Pre-Norman, Norman, Transitional, Early English, Decorated and Perpendicular periods. While the exterior of the lancet windows on the west front seems plain by comparison with other churches in Yorkshire, on the interior they are ornate and deeply recessed, superb examples of Early English architecture. The asymmetry of the church is caused by an intruding pillar on the south-west side of the central tower, visible in the nave looking east.

In some respects, Ripon's cathedral is more a parish church. It was accorded cathedral status in Saxon times, but this lapsed and was not renewed until 1836.

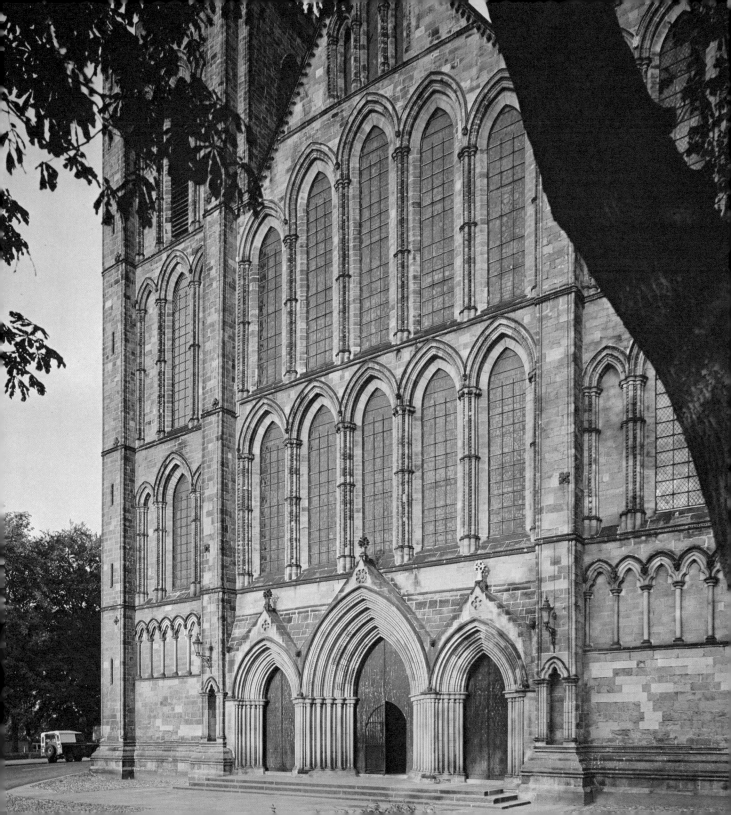

LANDSCAPE NEAR AYSGARTH

The stone walls and the Dales go together in most peoples' minds. To most they are an unusual and pleasant feature of the countryside. However, when you consider the time and energy that has gone into both their construction and their continued maintenance, then their significance is much increased. They offer a degree of permanence that could not be afforded by a hedge. They represent a profitable use of abundantly available local material. A glance at this picture shows that the hedge on the right hand, or northern side of the road is higher than that on the left. In fact, they offer a high degree of shelter for the barren upland area.

Aysgarth stands in the middle of Wensleydale, the only major Dale which does not take its name from the River, the Ure or Yore. Instead it is named after the village of Wensley near Leyburn.

But stone walls along the road side give one final clue to the nature of this countryside. The verges are narrow and pinched. It is as though the walls were driven to the very edge of the tarmaced road so ensuring that the maximum possible space is available to these rigorous upland pastures.

The typical stone field barns of this part of the Pennines, another relic of Norwegian Viking practice, offered both shelter for animals on the lower storey and a store for fodder on the upper storey, against the difficulties of transport in winter, though many are now disused.

While Yorkshire boasts no complicated lakeland network like that of Cumbria, yet water is indeed an important component of the landscape, whether in the broad placid rivers of the plains, the rushing streams of the uplands, in falls breaking through the limestone escarpments, or even in the form of the transient springs which burst out from the hillsides whenever rainfall or melting snow is heavy.

HARDROW SCAUR

Hardrow Scaur or Force, as the falls are often called, is the last leap made by the tiny mountain streams of Fossdale Gill and Herne Beck as they coalesce before joining the River Ure. The Hamlet of Hardrow shelters under the steep faces of Stags Fell.

Close by is Simon's Stone, High Shore, Bearsett, Shore Gill, Plough Wood, Pick Hill, and on the top Abbottside Common. Facing Hardrow is the town of Hawes above which is found Widdale Fell, Appersett Pasture, Back Sides, Gayle, Burtersett, Wether Fell, Dodd Fell. Roll these names around the tongue and think of them in a landscape of limestone screes, cliffs and scars, and green domed moors, sparkling fellsides, and everywhere rushing water.

Hardrow is spectacular. So is High Force in Teesdale. But so also are the successive falls of Aysgarth where the river broadens out over a series of ledges.

SWALEDALE

Swaledale is a different world from Wensleydale. Whereas most of Wensleydale is broad and open, and has rich pastures, the basis of its dairy industry, Swaledale is narrow and steep sided, given over to sheep farming and with only limited use for dairy products and the more usual breeding of 'store' cattle.

In Swaledale we reach greater and more exposed heights and once again we can see the patterns of the walls (this time in a snowscape). This re-emphasises the utility of the walls, which can form guidelines to lost travellers in a snowy world, and even more importantly, shelters against which man and beast can gain some faint hope of survival when caught out by a blizzard.

Swaledale's village names mark the path of a twisting road descending to the bottom of the valley, crossing and re-crossing the River Swale, from Keld through Thwaite, Muker, Gunnerside, Low Row, Feetham, Healaugh, Reeth, Grinton, and Marrick. Throughout this route the valley never widens, the steepness of the sides is never reduced, until finally along the well-wooded slopes near Marrick and Grinton, the Dale seems to make one last attempt to retain its isolation before the river quietly slides through a deep gorge into the plains.

RICHMOND

Guarding the gateway to Swaledale is Richmond, grouped round its magnificent castle. Here is one of Yorkshire's castles that never conceded defeat in siege or battle, since it was always considered too strong to attack! It soars above the town which clings to the slopes around it, huddling for protection perhaps against the marauding Scots.

It imposes its will completely on the Dales at this point. Even the river seems to tread deferentially in a wide swinging 'S' round its base.

Of course such a vantage point had to be a trading centre, and the main gates of the castle open onto a broad market place, around which are grouped the town's main shops, and in the centre of which stands an ancient church.

There are two churches in the town, so it is not surprising that one should have fallen into disuse in the present century. But here Richmond shows its military tradition, for the derelict church was seized upon as a fitting memorial to the exploits of the Green Howards Regiment, and has now been rehabilitated as a museum within which is a chapel provided for those old people who live round the square, and now find it difficult to make their way to the Parish Church which stands on a lower level.

LEEDS: PARK SQUARE

Let's be clear that Leeds stands in one of the Yorkshire Dales. The names Airedale and Calderdale may not be so familiar as Wharfedale and Wensleydale only because this part of Yorkshire proved conducive to the woollen textile industry. Water from the limestone country is hard. From the millstone grit it is soft. You cannot wash wool satisfactorily in hard water.

However, there was a vigorous life and well-developed communities here before the industrial revolution and their remnants may be found in the heart of the industrial sprawl.

Within a stone's throw of the classic Victorian Town Hall in Leeds, stands this gracious Georgian square. Now an elegant enclave of the legal and other professional offices, it is enclosed by modern arterial networks, including a motorway running under the City, and the typical tower blocks of modern city development.

The tower blocks are massed in the commercial centres of the city; the Victorian elegance of the shopping arcades in the city centre have been turned into pedestrian precincts. Traffic is being segregated. The City is indeed entering the twenty-first century with all the assurance of the city fathers, who were so convinced of their city's importance that in 1858 they got the architect, Cuthbert Brodrick, to design them the most impressive town hall in Britain (its dome is visible above the trees).

HAREWOOD HOUSE

John Carr was a famous York mid-eighteenth century architect and his influence on Yorkshire's architectural heritage is nowhere seen more clearly than at Harewood.

Carr was responsible for the great classical façade of Harewood, Adam for the interior and Capability Brown for the park. Thomas Chippendale, who was born at Otley a few miles from Harewood, is well represented by a magnificent collection of his furniture on display.

Work started on Harewood in 1759 and soon after it was occupied in 1772, the public was invited to view the interior, by appointment, on Saturdays between 11 a.m. and 4 p.m. From the first, this was a home which the Earls of Harewood were prepared to share with others as much for the fine collections of furniture, paintings, textiles, china and silverware as for the state rooms and exterior. Though the policy was reversed in the nineteenth century, Harewood now receives thousands of visitors each year.

The house, like so many in Yorkshire, stands on an escarpment in such a way that it takes advantage of the gentler southward slope. It is close to Wharfedale and midway between Leeds and Harrogate.

HAWORTH PARSONAGE

The parsonage at Haworth, the home of the Brontës, is typical of this region in design and construction. Here the millstone grit gives place to finer sandstones. This is revealed in the courses of stonework which are narrow, almost slate-like in proportion, and the stone slates used on the roof. The regular grain of the stone is conducive to the embellishment on the corners of the buildings and the lintels of the windows.

The proportions are those of the late Georgian period. It is a fine example of one of the smaller town houses with which the region is richly endowed.

Local history records that the Brontës arrived in Haworth on foot with their possessions piled on two handcarts. The house is smaller than most visitors expect and its furnishings remain largely as the Brontës left it. Even without its literary connections, or the tragic history of the family, Haworth has enormous value for the way in which it depicts life in early Victorian parsonages, in a village so remote that a train journey involved a five-mile walk to the nearest station.

BOLTON ABBEY

The rich and powerful monasteries which thrived on England's medieval wool trade are naturally found in close association with Yorkshire's sheep-rearing regions, the Moors and Dales.

Because of their wealth, they were targets for every raiding band from the Vikings to King Henry VIII's commissioners. Hence, their sites were chosen to afford some protection, being hidden in valleys and remoter parts.

Although the King's commissioners succeeded where the Scots had failed and found the treasure quickly, their stones were not totally despoiled because no local community was large enough to need them all. Thus, Rievaulx, Fountains, Jervaulx, Whitby, Byland, and many more rich monastic remains are found in such delicate woodland settings as those of Bolton Abbey, where lower Wharfedale ends as the valley turns north.

Bolton Abbey's fortunes were closely linked with the great Yorkist Lords of Skipton, the Clifford family, and a disputed legend has it that Bolton was founded in the memory of a young Lord Clifford dragged to his death in the Strid, a raging torrent about a mile away, by his pet dog.

MALHAM COVE

Of all the limestone features in Yorkshire that show the subtle solvent effects of running water on a seemingly hard rock, none surpasses Malham Cove.

Yet until comparatively recently there was doubt as to where the stream which helped to shape Malham came from. In limestone country the waterways have a disturbing habit of disappearing underground and one can never be sure which emerging stream derives from which stream that disappears, a characteristic which makes for the popularity of potholing. Thus, though it is logical to believe that the stream from Malham Tarn, a lake within a nature reserve above Malham Cove, is the one issuing from the base of the cliff, it has been found that the two have no connection.

Limestone country is full of surprises, from such precipices as Malham Cove and Kilnsey Crag in Wharfedale, to the awesome Gordale and the stalagmites and stalactites of Stump Cross underground caverns.

No less surprising are the steep-sided valleys at higher levels, with perfectly formed but completely dry stream beds. The striking thing about them is their silence. One expects but never hears the sound of running water: an eerie sensation. At the top of Malham Cove is a stream bed and there is no water – no waterfall – Malham Cove's last surprise.

THE COW AND CALF ROCKS

Not all the surprises are confined to limestone country. The millstone grit, sandstone and shale of Nidderdale, Blubberhouses Moor, Ilkley Moor and the southern Pennines have their fair share. The Cow and Calf Rocks at Ilkley, Almscliffe Crags on the opposite side of Wharfedale, Brimham Rocks near Ripon and Ripley, and Hardcastle Crags near Hebden Bridge owe much to the Ice Age. During succeeding waves of ice development, huge blocks were left precariously balanced on the ice. Others were carried by the ice and both were dropped when the ice melted.

The Cow and Calf (here illustrated), a large and relatively smaller block nearby, were left in this way to form for present-day sportsmen a suitable practice stretch for rock climbers.

A favourite picnic spot, this is also the place where, in 1886, members of Halifax Church Choir, on a day's outing, composed the words of 'Ilkley Moor B'aht 'at'. It was a joke at the expense of a young courting couple in the choir and they sang it to the hymn tune 'Cranbrooke'.

SHEFFIELD: CHRISTMAS ILLUMINATIONS

Recent years have brought vigour and strength to the cities of West and South Yorkshire. Diversification of industry, clearance of poor housing and reconstruction of road systems are transforming the face of England's remnants of the Industrial Revolution. At the same time care has been taken to preserve the worthwhile parts of older Yorkshire, Sheffield's Abbeydale Hamlet, Leeds Corn Exchange, Hepptenstall village, and many more.

But they form a part of this element in a thriving new scene – smoke-free Sheffield, with its Crucible Theatre, modern shopping centre and hotels, here seen in the light of Christmas illumination.

Not all the architecture can be uncritically admired. Nor could much of the Victorian and Edwardian structures that have been cleared.

But once again, the region's progress is in step with its character, a character formed of history and environment which has to be understood to understand the character of a Yorkshireman.